foreword by Bear Grylls

The joy of camping out under the night sky has been a part of my life for as long as I can remember – and it's a priceless experience.

Nowadays too much of my 'camping' tends to be either halfway up a freezing peak or curled up with no tent or sleeping bag in a mosquito-infested corner of a tropical rainforest – both highly over-rated compared to a decent campsite! But whatever the place, the principle is the same: escaping the mundane, leaving behind the pollution, the noise, the masses, and finding oneself again in the simple bare necessities of life.

One of those bare necessities is, of course, good food. This book has a handful of pretty ambitious recipes, but most are simple, wholesome and unpretentious, designed to give the maximum bang with the minimum of fuss. And that's how camping should be, full stop. Simple, messy, honest, wild and fun!

Adventure comes in all shapes and sizes. But life has taught me that you don't have to scale the highest mountains or skydive from helicopters to experience nature at her best. It's so much simpler than that. Hiking across Dartmoor and camping out for the night with good friends; wild camping in Scotland for the first time; the warmth and crackle from a campfire; the sizzle and smell of a barbecue next to your tent. These are all magical moments.

Camping gives us experiences that money can't buy, good and bad. Our family still laugh at the time when I was a kid on a family camping trip, it rained solidly for a week, until finally our tent collapsed and we had to sleep in a six-inch deep pool of rainwater for three nights! But it's in these shared moments that we begin to really live.

I have also learnt that laughter matters more than smart hotels, watching shooting stars is better entertainment than a computer game and music round a campfire somehow always sounds amazing.

My Grandfather had a great way of expressing the simple beauty of nature: 'There is always music in the garden, but our hearts have to be very still to hear it.'

That's camping in a nutshell for me.

Bear Grylls, 2007

www.beargrylls.com

introduction

Hello. Welcome to the Cool Camping Cookbook.

We like to think there's something a bit special about cooking and eating in the great outdoors. Licking an ice cream while ambling along the beach, devouring salty fish and chips on a park bench, sinking your teeth into a burger in the back garden, sitting by the campfire toasting marshmallows – it's all good. There's just something about the air, the smells, the sizzles and the earth beneath our feet that makes everything taste better.

Here are a few recipes from the Cool Camping team to get you out of the kitchen and into the great outdoors. Cooking in the elements can be as straightforward or as complicated as you like, but we're simple, honest folk, so you'll find most of the recipes here extremely do-able. It's not about creating Michelin-star rated grub, or presenting perfect, airbrushed photos. We don't mind the odd mucky thumbprint on our sandwich or a little bit of grit in our stew – real life is muddy, and all the better for it.

The chapters are vaguely split into how you'll be cooking; with just one pot, on a barbecue or on a campfire. But there's also food for your mood, with sections on 'comfort food' and 'something fancy'. Many of the recipes are interchangeable anyway, which makes the whole chapter thing a bit unnecessary, but we had to break it up somehow!

The best approach is to flick through until you find something you like the look of. Then get out there and give it a go.

Over to you then, campers.

Shatterberry Jam

S.D.T

fartychokes

Cavia
tomato

preparation

It's an annoying word, we know. But preparation can mean the difference between tucking into a steaming hot plate of loveliness or gnawing helplessly on a carton of powdered milk. Some of our recipes would benefit from some prep at home, so set a little time aside before your trip if you can.

It's useful to have a rough idea of what you'll be cooking and to prepare and pack what you need. Making a few sauces at home (see p20) and spooning them into tubs or jars is also a sensible precaution, unless you plan on taking a food processor with you. If you don't make your sauces beforehand, pack a potato masher, which does the job of a food processor but is more satisfying.

Before we begin, a few useful things we have learned and would like to share with you:

- Sealable food bags are your friends.
- Don't forget to label food bags with contents, measurements, cooking instructions etc.
- Frozen meat and homemade meals are also your friends. As they defrost, they'll keep your coolbox temperature down.
- Herbs, spices and stock cubes transform your food – dispense as much as you need into food bags (yes, them again).
- Tinned tomatoes also come in cardboard packs, so ditch the tins to save weight.
- Pitta breads are basically flat-packed food. We love them.
- Some tasty treats prepared at home (p139, p141, p142) and shared around the campfire will always make you popular.
- While self-sufficiency is all well and good, nearby farm shops, ice cream vans and village pubs are not to be sniffed at. Buy local and cut the food miles.

the kit

Deciding how much equipment to take with you on a camping trip is a pretty personal thing. There are those who prefer to sustain themselves armed only with a sharp knife and a packet of matches – while others will think nothing of loading up a 4x4 with a crate of champagne and an impressive selection of mustards.

Whichever camp you fall into, you'll probably find this little checklist quite useful. Photocopy it or download it from www.coolcamping.co.uk and add anything else you think you need to it. If the worst happens and you forget something – well, you'll remember for next time. And if you find that taking an ice cream maker along wasn't really necessary, you'll be inclined to leave it at home for your next trip. Chop and change your checklist as you go – with practice comes confidence, comes expertise. Or something.

A handy checklist

Gas, petrol or gel stove
Barbecue
Campfire grill/wire rack
Charcoal
Firewood
Fire starters or newspaper
Pots and pans (don't forget lids)
Cooking utensils
Tongs
Skewers
A very sharp knife
Tinfoil
Tin opener
Bottle opener/corkscrew
Plastic mixing bowls
Mugs/cups

Plates
Cutlery
Oven gloves
Lighter and (waterproof) matches
Potato peeler
Potato masher
Pestle and mortar
Chopping board
Washing up liquid and brush/sponges
Tea towels
Bin bags
Plastic food bags
Coolbox
Thermos flasks
Weighing scales, if you're fussy about quantities

1　2
4　3

what to cook with...

Camping stove
Most campers make do with a trusty old stove (1), and it's amazing what you can get these little things to do – see our one-pot wonder chapter (p24) for inspiration. For longer trips, or if you go camping quite a bit, it's worth investing in a double-hobber, preferably one with a grill underneath (p156). And don't forget the gas refills.

Barbecue
In moments of weakness, it can be tempting to opt for a disposable barbecue from the supermarket or garden centre. These are vaguely acceptable if you're cooking something quick like fish, but they don't give out much heat or last very long. A better option is to use a portable barbecue – both gas and charcoal ones are readily available. But for maximum brownie points, build your own simple barbecue (2) with a bed of coals, and a few bricks or logs either side to support a grill. Somehow, food tastes better on a barbie you've built yourself. See p41 for more barbecue tips.

Campfire
The original and still the best way to cook, no question, but it does require a little effort. You'll need kindling to get the fire going and a good supply of logs to feed it. Cook over the flames with a big cast iron cooking pot, also known as a Dutch oven (3), or by plonking a special skillet thing (p68) over the top. Alternatively, wait until the fire has died down and cook directly on the coals, or place a grill over the heat to use as a barbecue. You can also pierce things on sticks and hold them over the flames, a timeless and sociable way to cook. See p63 for more on campfires.

Other stuff
We're big fans of the Cobb grill (4), a portable little thing that can be used for roasting, baking, frying and smoking as well as barbecuing. It's highly efficient, environmentally friendly and cooks everything to perfection. We also mentioned a Dutch oven above, which we use as a campfire cooking pot. This becomes a whole new toy when used in the 'proper' way – by placing around 20 hot coals on the lid and another 10 under the pot. This cooks everything evenly and opens up the possibility of baking at camp. For stockists, see p157.

foraging

Because we are but a swarm of ants on the surface of God's picnic blanket, here are a few words on enjoying the fruits of our abundant countryside (while avoiding any nasty stuff that could leave us blue and stiff with our legs in the air).

So what to pick? Well, in springtime, young nettle tops, wild garlic leaves and other spring shoots are a welcome addition to salads and frying pans. The summer months bring with them delicate elderflower leaves, and in late July and August all sorts of sweet, juicy berries to squish between our fingers. Wild mushrooms flourish in the autumn, bringing weird and wonderful smells to the cooking pot.

Seasonal and regional variations will determine what you find on your investigative rambles. So before setting off, take the time to do a little research and work out which particular local delicacies you'll be searching for.

Some important things to remember:

- Carry a reliable, well-illustrated plant and fungi guide – many plants have edible bits and toxic bits. Make sure your book tells you which is which. And if you're not sure, don't pick it.
- Sturdy gloves will protect your hands from nettles and thorns. And sticks are handy for pushing aside brambles and yanking down overhead branches.
- Hedgerows by busy roads or old industrial sites aren't places you want to pick food from.
- Don't be greedy – only pick as much as you need.
- Don't let dogs go foraging on their own.
- Don't disturb sleepy woodland creatures, birds' nests, caterpillars, worms, beetles or any other living things.
- Keep a little piece of your foraged plant or mushroom aside, so that if the worst happens and someone has a reaction, the culprit can be identified.
- Uprooting a wild plant without permission from a landowner is illegal. For more information, visit the Food Standards Agency website.

Good places to go for more information about foraging:

The Forestry Commission: www.forestry.gov.uk
The British Mycological Society: www.britmycolsoc.org.uk
The Association of British Fungus Groups: www.abfg.org
The Woodland Trust: www.woodlandtrust.org.uk
A man called Fergus, who's an expert forager: www.wildmanwildfood.co.uk

a note on behalf of Mother Earth

Warning: hippy alert.

It's simple really. The good, green Earth has been kind enough to give us all sorts of lovely things to enjoy like trees, hills, squawky birds, sea, sand and sunshine.

And in return, all it asks of us is that we take a little care of our surroundings. So keep it green, people.

- Leave every site just as you found it.

- Don't wash dirty pans and plates in running water – instead, wipe them first with a biodegradable detergent, and then with a damp cloth.

- Take every last bit of rubbish with you – bottle tops, tin lids, scrappy bits of foil, cigarette butts, dead matches etc.

- Pop any leftover food in a bin bag to throw away later – don't just sling it on the grass. Hedgehogs probably shouldn't be eating ratatouille.

- If you find an ecological wonder like a nest, warren or den, by all means point and stare at it, but do not touch, poke or in any way harass it.

- Don't carve your initials into an unsuspecting tree. Give it a hug instead.

super-quick sauces

Cooking in the outdoors is all about getting the maximum flavour from your food with the minimum of effort. These tasty sauces can be knocked up in a flash and are extremely versatile – use them as dips, marinades or pour-over sauces. If you're feeling organised you could make them at home and bring them in a jar, but where's the fun in that? Master just three or four of these sauces, and you'll find cooking at camp an absolute breeze.

olive tapenade

ingredients

1 tbsp of capers
125g black or green pitted olives, chopped
3 anchovy fillets, chopped
1 garlic clove, peeled and crushed
1 lemon (juice only)
1–2 tbsp of olive oil

method

Mush all the ingredients together in a pestle and mortar until you get a smooth paste. Season as required.

ideal for

Bruschetta (p97) with a difference
Adding to barbecue fish or chicken

pesto

ingredients

1 garlic clove
Handful of basil leaves, chopped finely
Handful of grated parmesan cheese
2 tbsp olive oil
Handful of pine nuts
A sprinkle of pepper

method

Pound the garlic and basil together. If you don't have a pestle and mortar you can make do with a potato masher. Add some grated parmesan cheese, a dollop of olive oil and the pine nuts and mix to a smooth consistency. Season with pepper.

ideal for

Bruschetta (p97)
Bags of salmon (p53)
Extra Calzone filling (p73)
BBQ chicken fillets – slashed diagonally with the pesto sauce smeared all over, wrapped in foil and placed on the BBQ. Or if you are stuck, add to a saucepan of cooked pasta and top with cheese.

minty raita

ingredients

1 small carton of natural yoghurt
2 tbsp of organic mint sauce
1 tsp of turmeric
1 tsp of garam masala
1 tsp of chilli powder
1 tsp of salt

method

Pour the yoghurt into a bowl, add the mint sauce then give it a stir. Then add in the spices and mix thoroughly.

ideal for

Lamb chops with couscous (p121)
Spicy lamb kebabs (p57)
Paneer and vegetable kebabs (p128)
Dip for any barbecued meat or fish.
Or this makes a nice snacky dip with crisps or crudités.

lemon and garlic mayo

ingredients

150ml of good quality mayonnaise
1 lemon (juice only)
1 garlic clove peeled and crushed (optional)

method

Mix all the ingredients together and keep cool. Like the Fonze.

ideal for

Any fish dish (p53, p46, p110 & p113)
Corn on the cob (p54)
Or use it for dipping in chips from the local chippie.

mango salsa

ingredients

1 mango, ripe, peeled, stoned and diced
1 lime juiced
1 red chilli diced
2 spring onions trimmed and finely chopped
handful of coriander chopped

method

Mix all the ingredients together and serve with fish (as above) or fish cakes (p33).

beer marinade

ingredients

½ diced onion
½ diced green pepper
½ diced red pepper
½ diced yellow pepper
½ peeled and diced cucumber
2 tbsp of olive oil
10 tbsp beer
Salt and pepper

method

Mix all the ingredients together in a bowl.
Er, that's it.

ideal for

Chicken or pork; use as a marinade, then
barbecue in foil.
Or serve as a dipping sauce with
barbecued chicken or pork.

thai green curry paste

ingredients

A bunch of spring onions
1 birds eye chilli, de-seeded
A thumb of root ginger, peeled
1 lemongrass stem (remove the outer
  leaves & chop into 3–4 pieces)
1 big handful of fresh basil
2 big handfuls of fresh coriander
Zest & juice of 1 lime
A big slug of olive oil
A pinch of sea salt & black pepper

method

Ideally, you'll make this one at home and
take with – just whack everything in the
food processor and press the button.
Once it's smooth and pastey, spoon into a
plastic food bag and keep cool until
you're ready to use it. If you're making
this at camp, chop everything up as small
as possible and mush together with a
pestle and mortar or potato masher.

ideal for

Fireside fishcakes (p33) and thai green
curry (p77).

one-pot wonders

Hardcore campers compete to reduce their kit to the bare minimum, using titanium spoons and cutting off cup handles to save a few grams. But having a very basic kit doesn't mean you need to survive on mud and willpower alone. Try some of these frill-free recipes that'll give you bags of flavour from a little rucksack.

porridge

Porridge is brilliant fuel for the wood burner of your soul – bung in all sorts of tasty things to liven it up and you'll have enough energy to climb a tree and throw coconuts at your friend's head all day long.

Serves 1–2

ingredients
1 cup oatmeal
2 cups water
1 cup milk
Raisins
Toasted almonds

Optional extras
1 banana, peeled and sliced
A fat trickle of maple syrup or honey
Brown sugar
Blackberries, blueberries, raspberries, strawberries

method
Mix the oatmeal, water and milk together and bring to the boil. Simmer and stir – as it starts to thicken, add the raisins and almonds. Turn the heat off once the porridge has thickened. Stir in your chosen topping and enjoy while steaming hot.

mermaid omelette

Omelettes are the ultimate in fast food. They're quick, easy, tasty and full of eggy goodness. Best of all, you can plonk whatever you like in them, so your ingredients list can vary quite a lot. Well, apart from the eggs bit; they're pretty crucial. This recipe is quite over the top, but will impress even the most jaded omelette gourmet.

Serves 1

ingredients

2 eggs
50g smoked salmon
Handful of strawberries
1 tbsp chopped parsley or basil
Olive oil

method

Crack the eggs into a large mug or bowl and whisk with a fork. Slice the salmon, quarter the strawberries and add them to the egg mix. Add the parsley or basil, a good grind of salt and pepper and give everything a stir.

Pour the lot into a hot frying pan with a tablespoon of oil. Once the bottom solidifies, tilt the pan around to let the runny mixture get exposed to the heat.

Wait until the omelette loosens from the bottom, then fold it in half and serve. Eat piping hot, with a glass of Bucks Fizz if you're feeling fancy.

ramen noodle soup

This stuff is hot, filling and delicious; the chilli gives it a kick that warms you up from the inside. And it's a one-pot dish, so there's less to clean. Bonus.

Serves 1

ingredients

1 steak fillet
1 beef stock cube (or chicken stock for a lighter flavour)
1cm square fresh ginger
1 red chilli
1 cake of dried noodles
3 spring onions
Small handful of mange tout
Small handful of beansprouts
Small handful of coriander
1 lime

method

Cook the steak over a hot heat for a short while so that it is well browned on each side, then put aside and allow to cool. Boil up some water and add the stock cube. Peel and dice the ginger finely, thinly slice the chilli and add both to the boiling water with the noodles. Stir the noodles to help them break up.

Slice the spring onions and add. When the noodles are nearly cooked, add the mange tout and beansprouts. Bring to the boil, then turn off the heat. Slice or shred up the steak and mix it into the soup with some lime juice and chopped coriander. Taste and season.

Serve from the pot or in a bowl with some extra slices of steak on top and a little sprinkle of extra coriander. Be sure to slurp up the broth as well as chomping on the noodles.

fireside fishcakes

Fishcakes can be packed with flavour and are simple to make. It's easier to prepare the mix at home and squish them into shape when you're ready to cook, but you can also make these at camp if you have a potato masher. Thai green curry paste will give these an exotic zing and save you having to find fresh lemongrass in the rural wilderness.

Serves 2

ingredients

250g salmon fillet (skinless)
3 tbsp Thai green curry paste
  (see p23 if you want to make your own)
1 spring onion
Handful fresh coriander
1 large or two small boiled potatoes

1 egg yolk
Freshly ground salt and pepper
1 lime
Breadcrumbs
Rice, limes and mango salsa to serve

method

Roughly chop the fish and potatoes and blitz in a food processor (or squash with a potato masher) until it reaches a smooth consistency. Stir in the curry paste. Slice the spring onion, chop the coriander and mix together with a little salt, pepper and the egg yolk. If it looks too dry, squeeze in a bit of lime juice. Sling the whole lot in a food bag and keep cool until cooking time.

When you're ready to cook, divvy up the mix and roll into golf ball shapes. Coat the balls in breadcrumbs and squish them into patties. Gently fry on each side for a few minutes – don't hassle them too much or they may break apart. When they're cooked through, squeeze over with lime wedges and serve with hot rice and mango salsa (p22).

> **Important fishcake information!**
> If you're making the mixture beforehand, note that it should be kept as cool as possible, preferably refrigerated. You could always freeze the mix to keep it cooler for longer, if you wanted to be clever about it.

caring, sharing soup fondue

Festivals. Parties. Football. Sex. Some things just get better when more people are involved. This is a really communal, let's-all-huddle-around-the-fire kind of recipe. Rather than the traditional cheese or oil fondues, you use stock as your cooking fluid, dunk in all sorts of savoury treats, and then drink up the broth.

Serves 4

ingredients

Various vegetables to dunk: try courgettes, broccoli, new potatoes, asparagus
4 chicken breasts
1 lemon
2 litres chicken stock
1 onion, quartered

method

Cut the vegetables into bite-sized pieces and arrange on a plate.

Slice the chicken thinly, squeeze over the juice of a lemon and grind on some fresh black pepper.

Put the stock in a big pan, add the onion and chicken breast pieces, bring to the boil and simmer. Now let everyone spear veggies from the plate and dip into the stock to cook. You might want to have a few extra fondue forks so you can have two things on the go at the same time. Try not to fight over snagging the tasty chunks of chicken that should be floating about in the broth. When all the veggies and chicken have been scoffed, drink the hot soup, which should have absorbed the added flavours. Some crusty, buttered bread would top it all off a treat. Anyone for a round of 'Kumbaya'?

> **top tip:**
> If you don't have fondue forks, cut the bark off some sticks, sharpen them up and get jabbing.

ratatouille

And lo, it was deemed that along with crisp sandwiches and vodka jelly, every student in the known universe would subsist on ratatouille until the end of term time. But this humble dish can actually be hugely satisfying, as long as it's left to burble away on a low heat for a decent amount of time. Maybe play a game of charades while you wait.

Serves 2

ingredients

1 red onion
1 tbsp olive oil
1 red pepper
A couple of garlic cloves
1 tbsp Herbes de Provence
Some fresh, local veggies
1 tin chopped tomatoes
A glass of red wine
2 tbsp tomato puree
Fresh, dunkable bread

method

Slice the onion and soften in some olive oil. While this is cooking, slice the pepper and add to the pan with a little salt and pepper. Squish a couple of cloves of garlic and add to the pan, along with the Herbes de Provence. Now would also be a good time to add any extra vegetables – courgettes and carrots both work well. When everything starts softening nicely, chuck in the tomatoes. Add a heavy-handed glug of red wine and the tomato puree. Bring the whole lot to the boil, then turn the heat down and allow it to cook for at least 30 minutes, stirring occasionally. Season with salt and pepper and any fresh herbs you have lying around.

Dunk in comforting wodges of buttered bread and eat while piping hot.

salami scramble

A hot, cheeky snackette best enjoyed on toast or stuffed into a pitta or bagel. The salami adds a satisfyingly salty, smoky edge – add some cheese to jazz it up if you fancy.

Serves 1

ingredients

2 spring onions
Butter
50g salami
2 eggs
A handful of parsley
A slice of bread

method

Sauté the sliced onions with a knob of butter. Chop the salami into chunks and add to the pan.

Allow the onions to soften and the salami to crisp up a bit. Then crack in the eggs and mix in with a touch of salt and pepper. Nudge them about in the pan over a low heat. When the scrambled eggs have set, chuck in some ripped up parsley, load everything on some toast and eat straight away while hot. Hurrah.

the barbecue bible

There's nothing quite like the sizzling sound of a well-oiled steak on a hot barbecue grill to drive otherwise reasonable human beings into salivating, primal meat-monsters. Grr. Ug. Grr.

Tips for successful barbecuing...

- Don't pitch your barbecue in a windy spot. Avoid being too near fences, trees, plants or buildings.

- You need to pitch on solid, even ground – the whole contraption must be stable.

- New barbecue? Let it burn off for a good ten minutes, and wipe the grill with a little oil. This'll stop food from sticking to the surface.

- Make sure all the food you want to cook is vaguely the same thickness, so they cook through at the same rate.

- Keep excitable children and pets well away.

- Keep a bucket of water or a fire blanket nearby.

- Don't let drunk people cook.

- Don't use liquid paraffin or alcohol to get the flames going.

- Special paraffin-free barbecue fire-lighters are available that won't make your food smell and taste horrible.

- Making your own barbecue? Use rocks, bricks or damp logs to mark out the area and contain the coals. Bricks can be used to vary the height of your grill, as the heat from the coals will vary.

- Wait until the flames have died down and the coals are white before you start cooking.

- A good way to check if it's ready is to hold your hand over the heat. If you can keep it there for 4 or 5 seconds, it's ready to cook. Any less, it's still too hot.

- If necessary, spread the coals around a bit before cooking to give an even heat.

- Once cooking, keep an eye out for hotter and cooler parts of the barbie and shift your food around accordingly.

- Some dried herbs scattered over the coals makes everything smell amazing.

Barbecue-starting for dummies...

If you're one of those people who can't get a barbie going with firelighters, try this method. Scrunch up 3 or 4 sheets of newspaper, pile then together and build a tipi of kindling over it. Light the paper, wait for the kindling to catch, then quickly add more kindling to feed the flames, leaving space between and underneath the wood for the air to circulate freely. Gradually start adding charcoal to the top – the trick is not to smother the flames but let them burn through the coals. If the charcoal doesn't catch this time, no offence, like, but you probably shouldn't be the person in charge of the barbie.

the gut buster brekkie

A cup of coffee and an argument with the bus driver may be a typical way to break-fast for most urbanites – but it really is the most important meal of the day when you've just peeled yourself out of a sleeping bag and feel a bit cold and stiff.

A simple fry-up, then – but this becomes a breakfast of champions if you can get hold of some organic bangers and bacon, not to mention a few fresh farm eggs, with wispy feathers still attached.

Serves 2

ingredients

4 top-quality sausages
1 tin beans
2 tomatoes (or 4 cherry tomatoes)
6 rashers bacon
2 tsp oil or butter
2 eggs
Bread

method

Get the fire going and a cuppa in your hand as soon as possible. The key to a great breakfast is patience, so nibble on a hunk of bread with butter and jam to keep you going – you won't be eating for a while yet.

Six items will be competing for space over your heat, so bear that in mind – makeshift tinfoil trays really come into their own here.

Sausages go on first; let them cook languidly over a low to moderate heat to get them gorgeously gooey and juicy.

Beans go on next. They also need a slow cook so you don't end up with boiling hot, sugary tomato sauce and cold, hard beans – find a cooler spot towards the edge of the barbecue to perch the beanpot.

Halve the tomatoes, coat in a little oil and pepper, and wrap each half loosely in tin foil. Pop each package, cut side down, on the heat. Cherry tomatoes can be left whole and carefully placed on the grill.

After the sausages have had a good 10–15 minute head start, nudge them to one side so there's enough room for the bacon.

Make little containers out of a double thickness of foil and pop a little oil or butter in each. When the fat gets hot, crack an egg into each and leave to cook on an idling heat.

Tear up the bread, toast and smother in butter. As soon as the eggs are ready, pile everything onto plates and add whatever seasoning or condiments you fancy.

Devour, stopping only to gulp down some more steaming tea or coffee.

catch of the day

So simple, but so satisfying – catching your own guarantees a succulent, fresh fish that will need little dressing or accompaniment. Pure, earthy, almost spiritual – this is the holiest of barbecue feasts.

Serves 1

ingredients

Some stonkingly fresh fish
Lemon
Fresh herbs (some thyme or a few bay leaves would be ideal)

method

Catch, gut and clean your fish. You could fry your fish in a pan with a touch of butter, but it's also tempting to lay it directly on the barbecue bars.

Once the bottom side has browned nicely, flip it over. You want the skin to crisp up and blacken with charcoal lines. Have a peek at the flesh – when ready, it should be firm and no longer opalescent.

Eat straight away while piping hot. While a scattering of fresh herbs would be welcomed here, they are by no means essential. Fresh lemon juice and a drizzle of olive oil or butter will give you all the sauce you need.

---

preparing your fish

Scrape the fish from tail to head with the back of a knife to de-scale it if required, then rinse. Cut along the length of the belly, open the fish and take out the innards, throat and gills. Use a spoon or the back of a knife to scoop up the blood vein from the backbone, then give the fish another good rinse. Done.

cool camping jerk chicken

This might just be our signature dish. Not because it's particularly original or fancy, but because we love it and cook it at every opportunity. It's a simplified version of a few different recipes given to us by various people, including Keisha. Hello, Keisha!

Serves 4

ingredients

4 tbsp of soy sauce
4 tbsp of Worcester sauce
4 tbsp of brown sauce
2 onion peeled and grated
1 green chilli (more if you like it hotter)
2 cloves of garlic, peeled and crushed
1 tbsp of brown sugar – demerara is perfect
Handful of thyme chopped finely
Pepper to taste
4 chicken breasts or thighs, de-skinned

method

Mix all the ingredients together in a bowl. Make slashes across the chicken breast to allow the flavours to soak in, then cover the meat in the marinade and place in a coolbox. Leave it for as long as possible to marinade.

When you're ready to cook, whack the chicken on a barbecue and cook evenly for around 20 minutes, turning regularly. Check the meat is cooked in the middle; when it is, serve with salad or rice.

bush burgers

Make sure you use decent organic minced beef for this one. Adding sausage meat gives a really juicy, succulent burger and big chunks of yellow pepper even make it look vaguely healthy.

Serves 4

ingredients

6 spring onions	2 tbsp of chopped flatleaf parsley
2 sweet peppers	4 slices mature cheddar cheese (optional)
1 tbsp olive oil	4 burger buns
4 sausages	8 rashers streaky bacon (optional)
200g minced beef	Salad, ketchup, salt and pepper

method

Slice the onions and dice the peppers. Soften them with oil over a low to medium heat, then set aside. Slit open the sausages and squeeze the meat into a bowl. Add the mince, peppers, spring onion and parsley and mix well. Then season well with salt and pepper.

Scoop out a little bit of burger mix and cook straight away to check the seasoning and adjust if required.

Now mould your burgers – the quantities here should make four fat, generous ones. Make a tiny hole through each patty. These will seal up when on the barbecue, but will ensure an even cook.

Put them over a medium to hot heat and cook, turning occasionally. If you're adding bacon, cook the bacon at the same time and set aside.

When the burger is nearly ready, lay on a slice of cheese. If your barbecue has a lid, pop it down for a couple of minutes to help the cheddar melt.

Meanwhile, toast up your buns and get some salad chopped – assemble your burger, topping with some salad, a slice of bacon and copious amounts of ketchup.

bags of salmon

Here's a delicious way to infuse shop-bought fish fillets with oodles of flavour. Barbecueing the salmon in foil 'bags' helps keep them juicy and succulent; just add one of the four suggested flavour combos for a taste sensation.

ingredients

1 salmon fillet per person, plus your choice of flavours

method

Make a secure bag by taking a large sheet of foil, folding it in half, then turning over the two sides to make a wallet. Season the fillet with a little pepper and pop it into the bag with your choice of flavouring (see below). Fold over the open edge to seal the bag, then barbecue over a medium heat for 10 minutes. Fish doesn't take long and it's important not to overcook it, so peek inside the bag to check if it's cooked. If it's not, leave for another few minutes. If it is, serve with some spuds and green vegetables.

Here are four ways to flavour your fillet – but feel free to experiment with interesting herbs and spices:

Fresh herbs and lemon:
Mix up 1 tbsp of olive oil, the juice of 1 lemon and a handful of fresh, chopped herbs like parsley, coriander, tarragon and chives. Add a little pepper and rub all over the fish. If you're out of herbs, a splash of white wine and a squeeze of lemon will work.

Garlic butter:
Blend some softened butter with finely chopped garlic and herbs. Wrap in foil and stick it in the coolbox. When set, add a couple of knobs to each fish bag.

Pesto:
Smear some homemade pesto (see p21 for recipe) generously all over the fillet.

Tomato and ginger:
Heat half a bottle of passata in a pan, grate in a thumb of ginger and add salt, pepper and a good pinch of sugar. Mix it all up, simmer for a few minutes and add to the fish bag.

corn on the cob

Did you know that the average ear of corn consists of 800 kernels, arranged in 16 rows? True fact.

Serves 2

ingredients

2 corn on the cob
2 tbsp olive oil
Handful of parsley
1 garlic clove, chopped
Salt and pepper
Butter

method

For the full barbecue experience, leave them in their husks and soak in water for about an hour – this stops them catching fire. Then peel back the husks but leave intact. Mix together the oil, parsley and garlic in a bowl and season with salt and pepper. Brush the mixture over the corn. Now, pull the husks back to cover the corn and secure with string if necessary. Throw them on the hot coals for about 20–30 minutes, turning regularly. If your cobs are husk-free, just wrap them in foil instead and cook in the same way.

Just before eating, slather on some butter and get chomping…

spicy lamb kebabs

These firey little kebabs are delicious when served with a Moroccan-style salad, toasted pitta bread and some tangy minty raita. The more aggressive among you may also wish to note that they are wonderfully aerodynamic, especially when forcefully propelled towards the rear of a sworn enemy you have spotted sauntering past your campfire.

Serves 4

ingredients

500g minced lamb
A large bunch of coriander leaves, chopped finely
1 onion, chopped into very small pieces
1 green chilli, finely chopped
2 garlic cloves, peeled and crushed
1 tsp turmeric powder
1 tsp mild chilli powder
2 tsp garam masala
1 tsp salt
8 wooden skewers (soaked)

For the salad:
4 vine tomatoes, diced
1 green pepper, seeded and diced
1 yellow pepper, seeded and diced
1 cucumber, peeled and diced
1 red onion, peeled and diced
1 tbsp of lemon juice
A few mint leaves, chopped finely
4 pitta breads

method

Thoroughly mix together the lamb, coriander, onion, chilli and garlic. Add the turmeric, chilli powder, garam masala and salt, and mix again.

Mould the meat into long sausage shapes around each skewer. Pop the kebabs on the barbecue and leave to cook, rotating occasionally.

While the kebabs are cooking, knock up a quick minty raita (see p22).

For the salad, put the tomatoes, peppers, cucumber and onion in a bowl. Stir the lemon juice and mint leaves together and drizzle over the salad. Toast the pitta breads and slice in half.

When the koftas are brown and sizzling, serve with the pitta, salad and raita.

pork and apricot kebabs

Lots of flavour for very little effort – if only everything in life could be as simple. This is a happy, sunny little kebab. If it had a name, it would probably be called Pam.

Serves 4

ingredients

500g pork fillet
24 dried apricots
Oil
3 tbsp honey and/or mustard
Rice, pittas and salad to serve

method

Slice the fillet into 2–3cm chunks and thread on a large skewer, interspersing each chunk with a dried apricot. Season with a little salt and pepper. Paint the kebab with a little oil as well as the honey and/or mustard. Place over a medium to hot barbecue. Turn regularly and brush with more honey every so often to keep it moist. You want the meat to be cooked through and the apricots to be nicely caramelised.

When ready, slide the pork and apricot off the skewer and enjoy with rice or pitta bread and salad. You could also try this with chunks of apple if you're not keen on apricots.

pork satay skewers

Peanuts and meat – who'd have thunk it? The fine people of the Far East, that's who. And how right they were.

The satay sauce is a little fiddly and needs to be made at home, in the presence of a food processor. This recipe also works well with chicken or beef.

Serves 4

ingredients

1 stalk lemongrass
1 medium red chilli
1 clove garlic
1cm piece fresh ginger
1 tsp ground nut oil or vegetable oil
1 small handful fresh coriander

2 limes plus extra to serve
225g peanut butter
200ml coconut milk
25g soft brown sugar
550g pork tenderloin
8 skewers (soaked)

method

To make the satay sauce, peel and finely chop the lemongrass. Chop up the chilli and discard the painfully hot seeds, then peel and finely dice the garlic and ginger.

Pour the oil into a saucepan over a medium heat. Add the lemongrass, chilli, garlic and ginger and sauté for a few minutes. Add the coriander stalks, the zest of 1 lime and the juice of 2. Stir fry for a few minutes, then add the peanut butter, coconut milk and sugar and mix until the sauce thickens.

Halve the mix. Chop the coriander leaves into one half of the mix – this will be the dipping sauce. Cube the pork and stir into the other half of the satay mix. (If you're making it early, pop this in a food bag to marinade, and keep cool, with the dipping sauce).

When it's time to cook, thread the pork onto skewers and smear with any remaining marinade. Place on a hot barbecue and turn occasionally until cooked through. Serve with the dipping sauce (hot or cold) and wedges of fresh lime.

campfire cuisine

Camping just isn't camping without a fire to warm your cockles, so light her up and try some of our fireside favourites. You'll find campfire classics alongside a few less-obvious recipes, but all taste sensational infused with flames and smoke you've created yourself.

First, a few words on campfire safety:

- Keep a shovel and a large bucket of water nearby.
- Build your fire at least 3m away from any trees, tents or undergrowth.
- Don't build a fire in the path of strong winds.
- Avoid loose clothing – a floppy sleeve will tempt flames.
- Never squirt liquid fuel on dying embers – unless you want to become a human firework.
- Keep your fire small and manageable.
- Make sure your fire is completely out before retiring to your tent. When it's died down, douse with water and stir with a shovel. Dig right into the centre and keep stirring until there's no more smoke or steam. Those hot coals are tenacious little buggers.

Right. Enough chat. Let's get building.

- Splinter two 30cm long pieces of wood into a pile of kindling.
- Pile up a mound of shredded newspaper.
- Construct a tepee around the paper with the kindling.
- Lay over some light, dry branches, maintaining the tepee shape.
- Strike a match and touch it to the newspaper.
- Let the flames catch the kindling and then the dry twigs. Add a few more little twigs here and there.
- Gradually feed the fire with successively larger bits of wood. Go easy. Don't block air circulation by chucking a great big log on top of everything.
- Rejoice! For man hath created fire!
- To cook in or over the fire, let the wood burn down to a hot charcoal bed first. This should take about an hour.
- There will be hotter parts and cooler parts of the fire. Get to know which these are to help you expertly control your cooking times.

Most of the food in this section can sit straight on the coals of the fire, but a skillet (p68) over the flames will give you more options. Adding a grill will allow you to tackle all the recipes in the barbecue chapter on your campfire and with a big cooking pot or a Dutch oven (p15) there's no limit to what you can do.

sausage on a stick

The title says it all, really. But on a related note, did you know that 'pigsticking' was a blood sport popular in the early 1900s, where hunters with big moustaches on horseback galloped about spearing wild boars? Robert Baden-Powell, godfather of the boy scouts, was a big fan, apparently. Dib, dib, dib…

ingredients

Sausages
Bread
Sticks

method

Find a stick. Make sure it's long and thick enough to be used as a toasting fork. Peel off the bark and sharpen the end. (You can also use wire or an old coat hanger to wrap around your stick and double up on the sausages.)

Skewer your sausages and make sure they're well secured. Wipe the sausage with a little oil and hold over the fire. Keep turning regularly, until the snag is nicely browned and cooked through. Don't hold it too close to the flame or it will burn before it is cooked – be patient. When ready, use a slice of bread as an oven mitt to slide off the sausage, cover in ketchup and devour.

baked potatoes

Aah, nothing like a steaming, buttery spud to lift any fireside meal from the desperate to the divine. Potatoes on the fire always take longer than you think, so get 'em on early.

Serves 4–8

ingredients
8 small to medium potatoes
Salt
Butter
Fillings of your choice

method
Wash the potatoes, sprinkle lightly with salt and wrap individually with a double thickness of foil.

Place the potatoes in the embers and turn regularly for about 40 minutes until cooked. Obviously, this will vary hugely depending on the size of your spud and how hot your embers are.

When cooked, carefully unwrap, cut open and fill with obscene amounts of butter and salt.

And of course add any other filling you like – grated cheese, baked beans, smoked fish, chilli con carne…

skillet fajitas

Don't worry, readers – 'skillet' is just American speak for a frying pan or wok. They use lots of odd words, don't they? Like 'sidewalk', 'eggplant' and 'fanny pack'. Think of some more while you're knocking up these rather fine fajitas.

Serves 4

ingredients

Olive oil
1 bunch of spring onions, sliced
2 red peppers, sliced
2 yellow peppers, sliced
4 chicken fillets
Pinch of paprika
Garlic
200g mature cheddar cheese, grated
1 small pot sour cream
12 soft tortillas

method

For campfire frying, you'll need a cast-iron skillet with legs to plonk over the flames (see p156 for stockists). Oil the skillet, then cook the onions and peppers over a medium to hot fire for a few minutes. Slice the chicken and add it along with a good pinch of salt and pepper. You could add some paprika and chopped garlic at this point, too.

Heat until the chicken is thoroughly cooked through and the onions and peppers are caramelised. Keep aside, and heat up a tortilla in the pan. When it bubbles up, add some of the chicken mix, a good sprinkling of cheese and a dollop of sour cream. Fold over and eat straight away while good and hot. Like, awesome!

sweet stir-fry

Stir-frying food requires heat and speed – you can add practically anything to this recipe and it'll taste great. (Apart from hedgehog, which will just give you a nasty case of 'spiny tummy'.)

Serves 4

ingredients

Olive oil
1 bunch of spring onions, sliced
2 sweet peppers, sliced
200g pork tenderloin, cut into medallions
2 tbsp soy sauce
2 tbsp honey
200g mange tout

200g fine green beans
200g bean sprouts
A handful of chopped herbs:
    coriander, parsley, chives etc
2 lemons
4 cakes of dried noodles

method

Get your skillet or chosen pan (and it should be the biggest you've got) over the fire so it's super-hot. While it's heating up, prepare your ingredients so you don't waste any cooking time. You want every ingredient you add to fry quickly, as opposed to a languid sauté. This means you may need to stir-fry each item individually, so have a warm bowl or dish handy to keep each item in when cooked.

Get your oil hot, and throw in the onions. Keep them moving in the pan. Then the peppers – make sure they start to really colour. Now chuck in the pork, soy sauce and honey (dispense the veg into another pot or bowl if necessary). When the pork seals, add the mange tout, beans and a little more oil. After a minute or two, add the bean sprouts, herbs and lemon juice. Return any 'resting' veg to the pan and give everything a hot, fast stir.

Serve on a bed of boiled noodles, adding more soy sauce as required. Some chilli sauce would give it a welcome kick, too.

calzone

OK, so it's not exactly how Mama used to make – but then Mama probably had a well-stocked kitchen, a large wine cellar and a goat called Alfredo tied to a lemon tree to help her. Pah.

Serves 4

ingredients

Ciabatta bread mix
Olive oil
1 bunch of spring onions
1 tin tomatoes
Tomato puree

1 glass red wine
2 tbsp Herbes de Provence
150g ham
150g mature cheddar
150g mozzarella

method

Unforgiving foodies may insist on crafting their own handmade pizza dough, but in the wilds it's a little trickier. Life is short, so go with the packet of bread mix.

Make according to pack instructions, and allow to rest.

Meanwhile, make the sauce. Simply chop the onions and fry in some olive oil. When softened, add the tinned tomatoes, a good squeeze of tomato puree and a splosh of red wine. Sprinkle with herbs, bring to the boil and allow this to simmer until it thickens up.

When the dough is ready, roll out a flat circle about 20 to 25cm across. An unopened or empty wine bottle makes a perfect makeshift rolling pin. Take care not to roll the dough out too thin – you don't want it to break after you add the filling.

Spread a good dollop of tomato sauce over the pizza, add some chopped ham and grated cheese (half cheddar, half mozzarella), then season with salt, pepper and some herbs. Fold in half and seal up the edges, so it looks a bit like a Cornish pasty. Sprinkle some flour on a double thickness of foil and wrap up your calzone.

Rake the coals to give you a good flat layer and place the calzone on top. Cook for about 10–15 minutes, turning occasionally. Unwrap from the foil and enjoy, taking care not to burn yourself – the filling will be really hot.

Other fillings? Try chucking in a raw egg, mushrooms, chicken, olives, peppers… whatever you fancy, really.

building a tripod

The traditional way to support cooking pots and kettles over the campfire is to dangle them from a tripod. Making your own is easy if you have the raw materials to hand – and you'll look like a campfire expert! It's a blatant glory job, but it might just get you out of the washing up.

You'll need three strong branches or bits of wood, at least 1.5m long, and all roughly the same length. Lie two together on the floor in a tent shape with the top bits overlapping a small way, then bang a nail through the bit where they overlap, to secure them.

Stand them on end with the short bits sticking skywards, then use the third branch to complete the tripod, leaning it against the v-shape and tweaking the angles until it feels solid and secure. You can bang in another nail if you like, but either way, some string or twine needs to be wrapped around the join until you're sure nothing will budge. (If you don't happen to have a hammer and nail to hand, just use the string, but tie it extra tight).

Before placing your finished tripod over the fire, douse it with a bucket of water to protect it from the flames.

To support the cooking pot, you can either hang a length of chain from the centre of the tripod or use another length of wood. For the wood option, measure the drop from the centre of the tripod to the point at which you'll be hanging your pot. Don't forget to allow for the height of the campfire, the flames and the full depth of the cooking pot and handle. Your piece of wood should be longer than this, to stick out of the top of the tripod. Carve a good, big, angled notch out of the wood for the pot handle, then double-check the length before securing it to the top of the tripod with string.

For heavier pots, you may want to carve another notch at the top of the piece of wood; you can then feed the string through this notch when you secure it to the tripod, to stop it from slipping down into the fire.

thai green curry

A fragrant, perky dish – perfect for getting you out of the doghouse if you've been careless enough to be put in one. You'll need a nice big cooking pot to let everything slosh around and to give everyone a go at stirring.

Serves 4

ingredients

250g rice
Groundnut or vegetable oil
1 tbsp Thai green curry paste (p23)
2cm cube of peeled fresh ginger
1 red chilli
1 bunch spring onions
2 sweet peppers

2 courgettes
100g cherry tomatoes
2 tins coconut milk
250g tiger prawns
3 lemons or limes
A big handful of fresh coriander
Limes to garnish

method

First, put the rice on to boil. Once it's simmering away, turn your attention to the curry.

Get a big pan, cooking pot or Dutch oven, add a good splash of oil and put over a medium heat. Add the curry paste, the finely diced ginger and the diced chilli. Slice and add the spring onions. Slice the peppers, add to the pan and allow them to soften.

Slice the courgettes and add to the pot, along with the cherry tomatoes. When the peppers have started to brown and the onions have softened, add the coconut milk and the prawns. Squeeze in the juice of the lemons or limes and stir well. Let this burble away for 5 minutes or so.

By now your rice should be practically cooked. Drain it, and add to the pot of curry. This will thicken up the sauce and allow the rice to really absorb the flavours.

When the rice is cooked to your liking, stir in some chopped coriander, sprinkle with salt and pepper and serve.

lemon chicken tagine

Brighten up even the dullest outfit by tipping this yellowy, fragrant, spicy dish over someone's head. Erm, hang on… is that right?

Serves 4–6

ingredients

1 tsp garlic puree
Spices: (½ tsp black pepper, 1 tsp ground ginger, a good pinch of saffron,
  1 tsp cumin, 1 tsp turmeric, 1 tsp ground cinnamon, 1 tsp coriander)
Olive oil
2 chicken breasts
12 chicken thighs
2 onions
200ml water
250g couscous
A handful of olives
2 lemons

method

This requires a bit of at-home prep or an early start at camp. Mix the garlic with the spices and a tablespoon of olive oil. Take the skin off the chicken pieces and de-bone the thighs. Cut the chicken into generous bite sized chunks. Mix these well in the spice mixture and refrigerate in a plastic bag wrapped in foil, or store in a coolbox.

When you're ready to get cooking, heat some oil in a saucepan, Dutch oven or suitable tagine dish, fry the chicken over a medium heat until sealed, then add the onions and continue to cook until they sizzle. Then add the water, put the lid on and cook over a low heat for about 20 minutes.

While this is cooking, sort out the couscous. Put it in a bowl with a pinch of salt and pepper, cover with boiling water and wrap cling film over the top. After 5 minutes, fluff the couscous up with a fork until the grains separate. Add it to the chicken mixture and stir in, adding the olives and sliced lemons. Add more water or wine to get it to the consistency you want, heat through and serve.

the fire pit

The most primal of cooking methods, and a sure-fire way to convince friends and family that you're but one step away from becoming one of those self-sufficient types who can live off the land and fashion a speedboat from two small coconuts.

You'll need space, time, a spade, bricks, chicken wire and some willing helpers.

Oh, and you need to start the whole process a good few hours before feeding time.

method

Right. The first thing you need to do is dig a big pit.

The size of the hole you need is determined by the size of what you're going to cook. The pit needs to be about 30cm larger in every direction than your total food area. Try a metre long and about half that in width and depth. Set aside any turf or earth you dig up carefully (because you'll need to put it back).

Now line your pit with bricks or stones. Bricks are a better bet, as they won't explode like flint and limestone.

Now build a large, well-fed fire in the bottom of your pit to make your charcoal cooking bed. You'll need a lot of hot coals for this, so if you're organised, you will already have a fire on the go from which to scoop some burning wood and char-coal for your pit. Ideally, you want the hot bed to be about a foot deep.

While the fire's burning down (it should take about 3 hours), sort out the food you want to cook. You can be as ambitious as you like (we tried a duck stuffed with orange slices), but if it's your first time, go for uncomplicated stuff like a whole chicken, a juicy ham, a leg of lamb or hunks of beef. Vegetables like sweet potatoes, corn on the cob and butternut squash also react well to pit cooking, as they are difficult to overcook.

Season your ingredients well and wrap them in a generous amount of foil. Then wrap the foil packages in a heavy layer of wet newspaper or straw – this acts as an insulator to stop your food instantly frazzling. Now tightly mould chicken wire round each package so you can hook your food up later without burning your hands. Once the fire has burnt down, carefully lower in the food packages. Quickly refill the pit with soil and earth – the idea is to block off any oxygen from the firepit to keep the food from burning. Mark the pit area with sticks so you'll know where to dig later on, and leave for about 10 hours.

When you come back to the pit, dig up the covering (you need to be wearing protective gloves or oven mitts of some kind here), scrape off the ash and fish out your bundles of chicken wire. Carefully unravel to expose tender, moist treasures.

Eat, enjoy – and possibly beat your chest.

Obviously, a huge array of factors can affect cooking time – the size of your ingredients, how hot the coals are – so expect a little trial and error. But just think, when you get really good, you can try cooking a whole hog like the Polynesians do. Sure, it might take a week or so, but you can have one heck of a party while you're waiting.

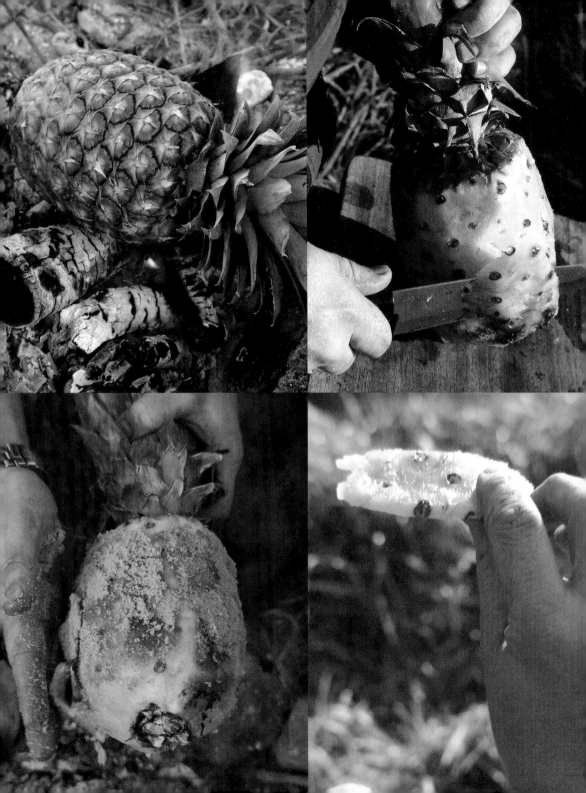

pineapple flambé

Popular beat combo Crowded House once sang a song called 'Pineapple Head'. We wonder if they wrote it after too many nights on the rum punch, because we're still not sure what they were singing about. Ponder this while you roast your drunken tropical fruit – answers on a postcard, please.

Serves 4

ingredients

1 pineapple
Rum or your favourite spirit
100g demerara sugar

method

Plonk your pineapple on a bed of hot coals, making sure you keep the leaves at the top out of the flames. Allow it to thoroughly brown all over. Then remove from the heat and carefully slice away the skin, taking care not to burn yourself.

Return the fruit to the heat, make sure everyone stands well back – and pour over a healthy glug of rum. Flames will go everywhere, so watch your eyebrows. When the alcohol's burned off, grab the pineapple, pat on the demerara sugar and return to the heat, turning regularly until the sugar caramelises.

Hoist the pineapple by its singed leaves and carve off hunks of sweet, golden, boozy fruit.

toasted marshmallows

Remember the scary marshmallow man who went on the rampage in popular motion picture Ghostbusters? He was set on fire and went all melty and gooey. Now you can recreate that very scene by the comfort of your own campfire. You be Dan Aykroyd, I'll be Bill Murray.

ingredients

1 bag of marshmallows

method

If you don't have metal skewers, find a stick, scrape off the bark and whittle the end into a spike.

Impale a marshmallow on the stick. Pink or white. Your call.

Approach the fire. Offer marshmallow sacrifice.

Sniff. Smell the burning sugar. Mmm.

Eat before the marshmallow completely melts off the stick.

Repeat, adjusting your preferred toasting technique as you go.

Try squishing them between a couple of digestives or ginger biscuits (see p139) to make a hot marshmallow sandwich.

banana flakes

When it comes to awarding the prize for best fruit ever, the banana comes pretty close. It's tasty, handily packaged and makes for a great comedy moustache. However, when God invented banana, he forgot to include one very important thing… the chocolate!

Serves 4

ingredients
4 bananas
4 flakes

method
Start to slice your chosen banana in half across its middle, but make sure you don't cut them right through. Snap a flake in half, and carefully push each half down the middle of each banana handle. Lots of banana flesh will burst out – ignore it. And if the banana skin splits here and there, don't worry.

Manoeuvre the banana halves back together as best you can. Wrap snugly in tinfoil.

Pop the bananas on the fire for about 5 minutes. Unwrap and scoop out the gooey, chocolately mess with abandon and delight.

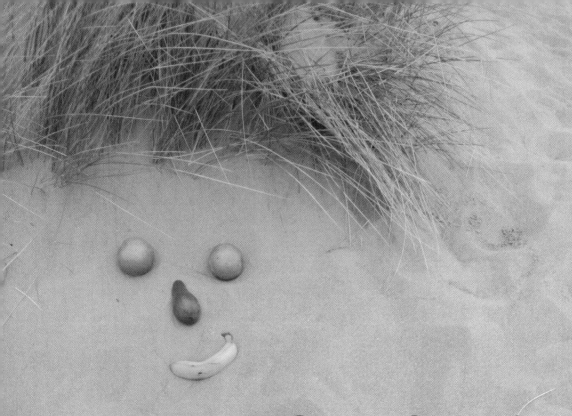

comfort food

Sometimes, you get one of those days when everything seems to go wrong. A gale force wind removes your hat. A goat nibbles through a tent pole. Your camping partner develops scurvy. You can't get that Westlife song out of your head. It rain, rains and rains some more.

These recipes are designed to give you a big, squishy hug when you're on the verge of burning your rucksack and heading for the nearest B&B.

swiss breakfast

This is essentially what our friends in the North refer to as a hash – a comforting mush of leftover flavours to get your day going. Do the Swiss actually eat this for breakfast? Sadly, none were available for comment at time of writing – but it would be nice to believe they do.

Serves 2

ingredients

3 spring onions
2 tbsp olive oil
4 rashers of streaky bacon
6 small, boiled potatoes
4 slices cheese
2 eggs

method

Dice the onions and pop them in a frying pan with some olive oil over a medium heat. Slice the bacon, roughly chop the ready-boiled potatoes and add to the pan with a good pinch of salt and pepper.

Cook, meld and squish the mixture about until the onions have caramelised, the bacon is crispy and the potatoes have browned.

Add slices of cheese, allow them to melt, and then split the whole lot between two plates. Fry up the eggs and balance on top of the mounds of hash.

Eat. Smile. Relax.

minestrone soup

This is less of a soup – it's more a big bowl of hot, chunky, steamy, vegetable love – if it could, it would probably drive a VW campervan and listen to Creedence. Yeah, man. And don't Bogart that celery.

Some farm-fresh smoked bacon and a topping of sharp, tangy parmesan should give this all the punch it needs.

Serves 4

ingredients

1 tbsp of olive oil
4 bacon rashers, rind removed and chopped (optional)
1 onion, diced
2 garlic cloves, peeled and crushed
1 celery stick, sliced
1 carrot, peeled and diced
1 courgette, diced
1 leek, sliced
2 tomatoes, chopped
500ml vegetable stock
3 tbsp small pasta shells
1 tin borlotti beans (other beans will also do)
Handful of chopped parsley
Handful of grated parmesan cheese

method

Heat the oil in a pan and add the bacon, onion and garlic. Sauté for a few minutes, then add the celery, carrot, courgettes and leek and give it a good stir for 5 minutes or so on a medium heat. Add the tomatoes, vegetable stock, pasta and beans. Bring to the boil and then simmer for 20 minutes. Season to taste.

Serve in a bowl, and sprinkle over the parsley and parmesan. You'll probably need some crusty bread on the side to dip, scoop and dunk with.

feel-better bruschetta

Is everything looking grey, drizzly and a bit miserable? Bring a little Mediterranean sunshine to your plate with a quick, but utterly comforting bruschetta. It's super-simple, but with some ripe, juicy tomatoes, fragrant basil and homemade pesto, this toasty treat is sensational.

Serves 2 as a serious starter or a light lunch.

ingredients

2 seriously good, ripe tomatoes
100g black olives (preferably ones that have been marinated in something exciting, like garlic or chilli)
Fresh basil
2 tbsp olive oil
Salt and pepper
Half a French loaf
2 tsp tapenade or pesto (for recipes see p21)

method

Cut the tomatoes in four, remove the seeds and dice the flesh. Take the stones out of the olives and chop them up any old how. Tear up the basil and mix everything together with most of the oil. Season with salt and pepper.

Cut off the knobbly ends of your baguette and slice the rest of it lengthwise so you have two, large flat pieces of bread.

Rub the cut side with a little olive oil and toast. Spearing it on a couple of sticks over some hot coals works just fine. Once toasted, spread the cut sides with a little tapenade or pesto. Then pile on the tomato and olive mix and devour, licking your fingers as necessary.

Chop and change your topping ingredients with anything you like – peppers, sliced ham, artichokes, grass… OK, maybe not grass.

spicy sausage penne

Wherever you're camping, you'll always be able to hunt down a sausage. They travel in packs and don't run very fast. If you can't find plump, juicy organic sausages from a nearby local farm, supermarket ones will do – but the thicker and herbier they are, the better.

Serves 4

ingredients

8 sausages (thick, herby and preferably organic)
Olive oil
2 onions, peeled and chopped
1 red chilli, chopped (optional)
2 cloves of garlic, peeled and crushed
A glass of white wine
Handful of oregano leaves, or 1tsp of dried oregano
700g passata, or 2 cans of chopped tomatoes
Salt and pepper
500g penne
Handful of grated parmesan cheese

method

Slowly brown the sausages over your grill, fire or frying pan. In another large pan, sauté the onions, chilli and garlic for a few minutes. Cut the browned sausages into bite-sized chunks and throw them into the mix with a splash of wine and the chopped oregano. Let everything bubble away for a few minutes.

Add the passata or tinned tomatoes and simmer for 20–30 minutes, stirring occasionally until the sauce thickens up. Season with salt and pepper.

Meanwhile, add the pasta to a saucepan of salted boiling water and cook until al dente. Drain well. Throw the pasta into the sauce and give it all a good stir, then serve up, with a generous sprinkle of grated parmesan.

Tucking into a bowl of this steaming hot stuff feels as lovely as a small elephant approaching you on a cold, windy hill to give you a comforting embrace and envelope you in his large, velvety ears.

dry-your-eyes daal

The theory behind this dish is that you boil up the lentils in a pot, and in a separate pan fry up all sorts of spices. Then you chuck the sizzling spices into the lentil sauce – a method known as 'tarka', 'tadka' or 'baghaar' in Indian and Pakistani cooking.

Serves 4

ingredients

Lentils: red or yellow
1 tsp salt
Pinch of turmeric
1 lemon (or lemon juice)
1 tsp garam masala
1 tsp chilli powder
Groundnut oil

1 onion, thinly sliced
1 tsp ginger: either ready-minced or finely sliced
1 tsp garlic: either ready-minced or finely chopped
1 tsp each of cumin seeds and mustard seeds
1 green chilli
Fresh coriander
Naan, pitta bread or rice to serve

Rinse a cupful of lentils three or four times and leave to soak for 20 minutes. The lentils will expand, so don't plonk too many in – it'll be trial and error depending on how thick or runny you want the daal to be.

Rinse again and add enough water to just cover the lentils. Add the salt, a pinch of turmeric and bring to the boil. Simmer and cover for 10 to 15 minutes.

With a wooden spoon, fork or other sturdy instrument, stir the swollen lentils into a mush. When smooth, start trickling in water, stirring constantly, until you get the consistency you want – 2 or 3 cups of water should do the trick. Squeeze in some lemon juice, a teaspoon of garam masala and a teaspoon of chilli powder. Simmer.

In a shallow frying pan, heat up a generous amount of oil (groundnut would be ideal). Add the sliced onions and fry until caramelised. Then add the ginger, garlic, seeds and a chopped green chilli. These need to really sizzle and colour – make sure the oil is as hot as possible.

When the seeds are popping and everything's looking golden, stand back a little and tip the frying pan contents into the pot of daal. It will hiss and steam at you. Stir the tasty stuff through the gloopy lentils. Adjust consistency by either stirring in more water, or cooking down to a thicker sauce.

Tear over some fresh coriander, and enjoy with toasted naan, pitta bread or rice.

camper's cassoulet

A rich, slow-cooked cassoulet, abundant with tomatoes, sausage, duck fat and beans, is the pride of many a kitchen in the south of France. Regional variations abound, each claiming to be more authentic than the other.

This, however, is a shockingly unauthentic version for you to hum and haw over as you sit by the fire. But it's dead easy, so is perfect for cooking on a gas burner. If you're preparing this at home to freeze and use later, or are just feeling flashy, by all means use confit de canard instead of chicken thighs.

Serves 6

ingredients

1 heaped tbsp of duck/goose fat
(olive oil will do if you're stuck)
6 skinned and boned chicken thighs
6 cooked sausages
5 cloves of garlic
250g chorizo sausages
1 tin of tomatoes

Tomato puree
1 glass white wine
1 chicken stock cube
800g tinned haricot beans
1 bay leaf
1 sprig of thyme
Fresh bread

method

Carve up the chicken thighs and fry in a little fat or olive oil. Slice the sausages, chop the garlic and add to the pan, adding more fat or oil as necessary to stop it sticking.

Throw in the sliced chorizo and stir.

Add the tinned tomatoes, tomato puree, wine, stock, beans (drained and washed) and herbs. Simmer for half an hour at least, stirring regularly. The longer you leave it, the tastier the stew will be.

Before serving, add any remaining goose fat to richen the whole dish up. Serve with big chunks of fresh bread.

roast chicken

This Sunday lunch staple is guaranteed to make everyone within sniffing distance go all misty-eyed and soppy. You do need a bit more kit for this but if you don't have a Cobb cooker (see p15) then a roasting barbecue with a lid will do the same job.

Serves 4

ingredients

1 medium-sized chicken
Olive oil
1 head of garlic
1 lemon

Herbs (such as thyme and rosemary)
1 onion
Vegetables (potatoes, green beans, parsnips, sweet potatoes, carrots)

method

Give the chicken a rinse and pat dry.

In a bowl or cup stir the olive oil with a couple of cloves of crushed or chopped garlic, a good squeeze of lemon juice and any herbs you may have lying about – fresh rosemary or thyme would be excellent, but dried Herbes de Provence will be fine.

Rub this oily, herby juice all over the bird – inside and out.

Pop half a lemon, more herbs and half an onion up the chicken's bum, and place in the middle of the cooker or barbecue.

Chop your potatoes, parsnips and or carrots into smallish chunks, give them a light coating of oil and arrange around the chicken with a few unpeeled cloves of garlic and any spare lemon or onion. After a final heavy sprinkle of salt and pepper, put the lid on for an hour and a half.

Occasionally lift the lid and shuffle a few spuds around to make sure everything's cooking nicely. Get your other veg – carrots, beans etc. – on the boil in the meantime.

After an hour and a half, pierce a chicken thigh with a skewer – if the juice that runs out is clear, the bird is cooked. If the juice is even slightly pink, pop the lid down and let it cook on.

When cooked, serve the chicken with the pots, roast onion and any other veggies you fancy. Don't forget to squeeze out the sweet roast garlic flesh, and fish out the hot lemon from the chicken cavity – the juices will give you all the gravy you need.

hot chocolate

Like a hug from Stephen Fry or a big-eyed dog proffering you his paw, a cup of hot chocolate can make you realise that life isn't all that bad.

Serves 4

ingredients

2 pints semi-skimmed milk
400g milk chocolate
A bag of marshmallows

method

Warm the milk in a pan, break up three-quarters of the chocolate into pieces and add. Stir regularly to ensure the chocolate lumps don't stick to the bottom. Pour into four mugs or glasses and top with a marshmallow or two. Snap the remainder of the chocolate into four long pieces and use them as naughty edible stirrers.

something fancy

A good way to cajole reluctant campers into enjoying themselves is to exceed their expectations. By serving up some lobster or a Sunday roast by the campfire, they'll see that cooking in the outdoors is not the preserve of strange men who collect roadkill. In fact, as these recipes prove, sometimes there's simply nothing posher. More champers, anyone? Chin, chin!

salt brick fish

This method may sound like utter madness but we promise it works and won't leave you with a stupidly salty fish supper. Trust us. We love you like you're one of our own.

Serves 2

ingredients

1 large fresh fish
2kg rock salt
4 egg yolks
Water
1 lemon or lime
Herbs and seasoning

method

In a huge pan or bowl mix the rock salt with the egg yolks and enough water to turn it into a congealed sludge.

Stuff your catch with a little lemon or lime, some fresh herbs and a grind of pepper.

Lay out a big double thickness of foil. Pour on a third of the salt. Lay the fish on top and then cover with the rest of the salt. Pat firmly together to mould into a salt brick, covering every last bit of the fish.

Fold over the edges of the foil and wrap into a bundle. Pop in a Dutch oven or lay straight over hot coals, covering with a few more. Leave for at least an hour and a half – if the fish is a real whopper, it may need longer.

When cooked, the salt should have hardened into a brick. Break open to find your fish beautifully moist and cooked through.

baked lobster

Just think, if you were a member of the Royal Family you'd probably be able to enjoy a plate of baked swan with some fricasséed peasant on the side. But you're not, so you'd better do with a spot of lobster instead.

Serves 2 as a starter or 1 as a main

ingredients

1 lobster
Butter
Lemon and garlic mayonnaise (p22)
1 lemon

method

Ideally, you'll be selecting a fresh juicy lobster from the quayside near your campsite. If you're bringing one from home, you're better off carrying a frozen lobster in your rucksack than a fresh one (or a live one, come to think of it). It'll defrost through the day in your coolbox – just make sure it's fully thawed before you cook it.

Cut your lobster in half lengthways, from head to tail. Get rid of the brown stringy bit that runs down the tail, the feathery gills and the little green stomach sac.

Brush the lobster halves with soft butter and put them, shell side down, on a grill or hot coals for 3–4 minutes. You'll know it's ready when one of its small legs comes off with a gentle tug.

An alternative cooking method is to place the whole lobster shell side down on the grill or coals. Wait until the shell turns bright red, then turn and grill for another 5 minutes. When cooked, cut and prepare the lobster as above.

Scoop out the white, sweet flesh and dip into the mayonnaise. Crack the claws with the back of a heavy knife and savour the contents. Above all, feel smug that you are enjoying such a stereotypically snooty dish in the great wide open.

seared tuna with rice niçoise

We'll have none of that tinned tuna here, sonny Jim. That's for your cats and office lunches and motorway service stations. We only do fresh tuna here. If it's sustainable, like.

Serves 2

ingredients

100g rice
2 hard boiled eggs
1 handful fine green beans
2 fresh tuna steaks
1 small handful olives
Olive oil
1 lemon

method

Start by boiling your rice and eggs – set both aside when cooked. Trim the green beans and cook lightly by plunging in boiling, salted water for a few minutes.

Brush the tuna steaks with a little olive oil, then sprinkle with freshly ground pepper. Sizzle over a hot barbecue or fry for a couple of minutes on each side, and then leave to rest.

Mix the rice with the olives, a tablespoon of olive oil, salt and pepper. Spoon onto serving plates, artfully scattering over the blanched beans and peeled, sliced eggs. Rest the tuna steaks next to the rice salad and serve with a squeeze of lemon.

mushroom risotto

Risottos soak up all sorts of flavours – so go heavy on the wine, fresh parmesan and herbs and keep a negligent eye on the clock.

Serves 4

ingredients

2 onions
3 tbsp olive oil
250g mushrooms (a variety will make all the difference)
250g arborio risotto rice
400ml white wine
800ml chicken stock
50g butter
100g parmesan
A handful of chopped fresh herbs
2 lemons
salt and pepper to taste

method

Slice the onions and soften in the oil. Hack up your chosen mushrooms and add – hopefully you've got a variety. Cook for a few minutes until the onions are softened and the mushrooms are browned. Season well with some salt and pepper.

Stir in the rice, cook for a minute or two and then pour in the wine. Bring to the boil and simmer, stirring regularly. As the liquid is gradually soaked up, keep adding chicken stock.

After about 20 minutes, the rice should be cooked and all the chicken stock soaked up – add more water if you need it. Stir in the butter, grated parmesan and fresh herbs. Season with fresh lemon juice, salt and pepper.

paella

As much a part of a trip to Spain as straw donkeys and sunburn, paella is best enjoyed in the sunshine with a jug of sangria.

Serves 4–6

ingredients

4 chicken thighs
1 chorizo sausage
Olive oil
1 onion
1 clove garlic
2 sweet peppers
250g mixed seafood (prawns, mussels, clams, squid etc)
200g paella or arborio rice
500ml chicken stock
1 tsp paprika
A pinch of saffron
White wine
4 limes

method

Chop the chicken and chorizo into bite-sized pieces and fry with oil in the largest pan you can find. Dice the onion and garlic and chuck in along with the sliced peppers. As the chicken browns, the onions and peppers soften and the chorizo goes crispy, now add the seafood. Stir this around so it seals and put to one side.

In a second pot, put the rice in with a tablespoon of olive oil and cook for a couple of minutes. Pour in the chicken stock, paprika and saffron. Bring to the boil and simmer, stirring regularly. The rice should start soaking up the stock. Add the white wine. When the rice has cooked, tip it in with the meat and fish. Stir everything well and bring the heat back up. Slice the limes and stir in – then serve up. Olé!

lamb chops with couscous

Couscous grains are quite tiny, measuring just 1mm in diameter once cooked. Which is small to us, but quite big from an ant's point of view. Think about it.

This delicious, colourful dish benefits from heavy-handed seasoning and a dollop of the minty raita on p22.

Serves 4

ingredients

4 lamb chops
2 tsp ground cumin
4 tsp garam masala
1 tsp salt
Olive oil
200g of couscous
1 red onion
1 chilli, deseeded

Handful of thyme
3 peppers: red, yellow and green
1 courgette
Handful of parsley
15 cherry tomatoes, halved
1½ lemons
Salt and pepper to season

method

Marinade the lamb chops with 2 teaspoons each of cumin and garam masala, 1 teaspoon of salt and a little olive oil. Leave to fester for as long as you can manage. Then barbecue to suit your taste – charred on the outside and pink in the middle suits us just fine.

Meanwhile, tip the couscous into a pan of boiling water – you want the water level to be about 2cm above the couscous. Cover for 5 minutes.

Pour some olive oil into a frying pan and add the chopped onions until they soften. Add the chilli, thyme, peppers and courgettes. Stir in 2 teaspoons of garam masala and let the vegetables brown a little here and there.

Add the couscous to the frying pan, season heavily with salt and pepper and mix thoroughly.

Add the parsley, tomatoes and the lemon juice. Serve up the couscous with the lamb chops and a dollop of raita.

sunday roast beef

As British as cucumber sandwiches and fights outside pubs at closing time, a roast beef dinner is the pride of the nation. This barbecue-based beef-fest is so special you'll want to take a picture of it to keep in your wallet.

Serves 4

ingredients

500g rib of beef
Salt and pepper
Herbes de Provence
8 shallots or 4 onions

12 medium-sized potatoes
4 courgettes
4 sweet peppers

method

Rub the beef with a little oil, salt and pepper and a tablespoon or two of Herbes de Provence. Start to slowly cook over a medium heat barbecue, making sure you keep turning it. Someone will need to perch near it for the next hour or so to keep it from burning or cooking too quickly.

Put the shallots on the barbecue and turn regularly until they caramelise.

Meanwhile, boil the potatoes. When cooked, drain the water and sprinkle the potatoes with a little salt. Barbecue these until they start to brown up and go crispy. Once the potatoes and shallots are cooked, put them to one side, wrapped in a dry tea towel to keep warm.

Chop the courgettes into 3cm sections and cook on the barbecue with the whole sweet peppers.

The beef is cooked when a skewer that's been pushed into the centre of the meat for 3 seconds is hot. Test it on the inside of your wrist. Once it is cooked, leave the beef to rest for about 15 minutes. In the meantime, pop the potatoes, onions, courgettes and peppers onto individual skewers and return to the barbecue to get them nice and hot.

Carve up the beef and enjoy with the barbecued trimmings – a little horseradish would top the plate off nicely.

a bit on the side

Whether you need a quick snack to keep the wolf from the door, want to add some extras to a barbecue or wish to extend a little hospitality after an unexpected visit from a large walking tour, here are a few extra recipes for you to enjoy.

bacon-wrapped asparagus

By selflessly bearing the brunt of the heat, the bacon protects and steams the asparagus, getting nice and crispy in the process. These are quick to cook, so you could probably get away with scoffing a few extra ones while nobody's looking.

Serves 4 as a starter

ingredients
16 slices of streaky bacon
16 asparagus spears

method
Wrap a slice of bacon around each asparagus spear, starting from the tip and diagonally winding down. You can do this beforehand, then wrap the whole bundle up with cling film and refrigerate or put in a coolbox.

Before cooking, wipe the bacon with a little oil, place on the barbecue and keep turning them every now and then.

They'll be cooked after about 5–10 minutes – the bacon should be sizzling and the asparagus tender, but not falling apart. These are especially good dipped in hollandaise, lemon and garlic mayo (p22) or a puddle of butter.

paneer and vegetable kebabs

Hailing from India, paneer cheese is a bit like mozzarella – but it won't melt during cooking, making it ideal for barbecues. We think it's a bit underrated, but once you've tried these barbecued cubes of cheesiness, there's no going back...

Serves 4

ingredients

1 tbsp of olive oil
1 lemon
Handful of basil, chopped finely
1 clove of garlic, peeled & crushed
Salt and pepper
8 button mushrooms
2 courgettes, sliced thickly

2 red peppers, deseeded and cut into quarters
2 green peppers, deseeded and cut into quarters
2 yellow peppers, deseeded and cut into quarters
2 red onions, peeled and cut into quarters
1 box paneer, cut into large pieces
8 wooden skewers (soaked)

method

Mix the olive oil and the juice of a lemon with the chopped basil and the crushed garlic. Season with salt and pepper. Place all the vegetables and the cheese in a bowl. Pour over the marinade.

Thread alternate chunks of vegetable and paneer onto skewers, using two pieces of cheese per skewer.

Place on the barbecue and turn frequently so the vegetables and cheese cook evenly. Brush the kebabs regularly with the leftover marinade. Once the veggies have cooked through and the cheese has browned, serve with barbecued meat, couscous or a salad.

hot halloumi salad

The mountain peoples of the remote Greek island of Gregoriakis greet the arrival of every newborn infant by constructing a giant ceremonial trumpet using only a mountain of halloumi cheese and a barrelful of chest hair.*

While that's all very well and good, we've decided to use our halloumi to make this hot and tasty salad instead. Though you could always build a mini-Stonehenge out of yours if you're bored.

Serves 4 as a side, or 2 as a main meal

ingredients

2 lemons
1 red chilli, de-seeded and finely chopped
Olive oil
1 packet halloumi
1 yellow pepper, seeded and diced
1 red pepper, seeded and diced
Mint, chopped

Thyme, chopped
1 pack of salad leaves – rocket is ideal
Handful of green or black olives
1 red onion, chopped
1 Lebanese cucumber, peeled and cubed
 (a green cucumber will do)
250g cherry tomatoes, halved

method

Squeeze the juice of one lemon into a bowl. Add the chopped chilli and the olive oil.

Cut the halloumi into slices and sprinkle the marinade over it. Leave it for 30 minutes or longer if you have time. Place the peppers and the halloumi onto the barbecue and turn frequently until the cheese becomes golden brown on both sides and the peppers turn a rich dark colour.

Leave to cool.

For the dressing, blend the chopped mint and thyme with a healthy slug of olive oil and the juice from your second lemon – add a grind or two of black pepper if you feel like it.

Mix the salad leaves, olives, onion, cucumber and tomatoes into a large bowl. Add the barbecued halloumi and peppers and give everything a light jumble. Drizzle over the herby dressing and serve.

*This is a lie. Sorry.

damper bread

This is unhygienic, unhealthy and horribly messy. The kids will love it.

Serves 8

ingredients
600g self-raising flour
100g caster sugar
A pinch of salt
100ml water

method
Mix the flour with the sugar and salt, and blend with some water to form a dough. Knead lightly until smooth, and allow to rest somewhere cool for 10 minutes or so.

Meanwhile, sharpen a long, sturdy stick, taking care to scrape off the bark.

Take a small handful of the mixture and squish it onto the end of the stick so it looks like a thick sausage.

Cook over the fire, turning regularly until it swells, browns and feels solid when you tap it.

Carefully pull the hot damper bread off the stick and fill the hollow with jam, butter, honey, cream, chocolate spread or anything else that takes your fancy.

garlic bread

Nothing gets folk salivating faster than garlic bread. If you wanted to, you could tie some to a long stick, wave it around and watch people scamper after it.

ingredients

150g butter
2 cloves garlic
1 small bunch parsley
1 loaf bread

method

Cream the butter in a bowl, squish in the garlic cloves, chop the parsley and stir in with a good pinch of salt and pepper.

Cut the loaf into thick slices and toast over a fire or in a frying pan. Once one side is toasted, spread generously with the butter and turn over to allow the butter to melt right through. Scoff while hot, crispy and dripping with garlicky goodness.

med veg

A sweet, colourful accompaniment to just about anything – enjoy on toast, stirred through pasta or with a juicy lamb chop. Cook these on-site or rustle them up beforehand and allow them to marinade in their own juices.

Serves 4

ingredients

2 red onions
4 sweet peppers
4 courgettes
1 aubergine
A head of garlic
Olive oil
Balsamic vinegar
1 small bunch of rosemary

method

Chop, peel and slice your various vegetables so that everything's vaguely the same size. Break the garlic head into cloves, but keep them in their skin. Coat everything with a generous amount of olive oil, a shake of balsamic and a scattering of chopped rosemary.

If time's on your side, you may as well barbecue everything. It's a bit fiddly and takes a while, but the veg will smell great and develop pleasing black char lines. Pop the garlic cloves on a little tinfoil tray so they don't escape through the wires.

If you plan on cooking this at home, heat a large baking dish in the oven at about 180°C with a generous splosh of olive oil. When it's hot, throw in all the vegetables and the rosemary. Mix around well and season with salt, pepper and balsamic vinegar. Cook for an hour, shaking the tray around every 15 minutes or so to ensure an even roast. Allow it to cool, then refrigerate.

sweets & treats

Would life be worth living if you couldn't settle down now and then to enjoy a biscuit, or maybe a cake, with a nice cup of tea? No, quite frankly. Now and then, you can't beat a bowlful of something sweet, sticky and possibly quite bad for you.

This chapter is vaguely split into two sections – the first few recipes are delicious things you'll need to make at home. And the rest are all goodies you can concoct in the wilderness.

giant ginger biscuits

A pleasingly portable snack that's as warming as sticking your head in a tumble dryer. Take our word for it.

Makes 6

ingredients

60g butter
75g caster sugar
185g golden syrup
2 tbsp treacle
3 tsp ground ginger
300g self-raising flour

method

Pop a saucepan over a low to medium heat and add the butter, sugar, golden syrup, treacle and ginger. Stir until the sugar dissolves and the butter melts. Remove from the heat and leave to cool.

When the treacle mix is at room temperature, stir in the sifted flour a little at a time. This will become pretty tough going as the goo stiffs up, but persevere.

Make pieces of dough the size of small oranges, roll into a ball, slightly flatten down and arrange on greaseproof-paper-covered trays. You may need a few trays, as you might only get one on each, depending on the size of your biscuits. If you are arranging more than one on a tray, leave about 5cm between the biscuits as they will expand. Bake in a preheated oven at 190°C for about 12–15 minutes until golden, then use a spatula to remove from the tray.

Cool on a wire rack, and store in an airtight container. Over time they may become a little chewy, but this is all to the good.

stickyfied goo-goos

Crazy name, crazy recipe. Seriously, the sugar buzz off these bad boys is enough to give you hairy palms.

Serves 8–10

ingredients
1 pack of butter toffees
1 pack of marshmallows
100g butter
3 handfuls puffed rice

method
Put the butter, toffees and marshmallows in a pan over a low to medium heat.

Stir regularly until you have a scary-looking, sticky mass. Pour in the puffed rice and mix together.

Using a wet spoon, dollop the goo by the spoonful into paper cases. Let them set in the refrigerator or coolbox and store in an airtight container. Don't stack them on top of each other, else it'll just turn into an unsightly mess.

When they are set you can eat, enjoy, run around a field whooping etc…

chocolate cement

This stuff has the power to turn cloud into sunshine, frowns into smiles and bad-tempered campers who've forgotten essential hair maintenance items into beaming, delightful outdoor companions.

Serves 4

ingredients

140g dark chocolate
4 egg yolks
185ml double cream
4 heaped tbsp cocoa
2 tsp orange zest

method

Break the chocolate into pieces and melt in a bowl. When it's nice and runny, beat in the egg yolks (make sure they're at room temperature so they don't cool the chocolate down).

Mix the cream, cocoa and orange zest together, beat until it forms stiff peaks and fold into the chocolate. Pour the lot into a container and refrigerate for a good 12 hours before you need it.

This'll leave you with a solid dishful of chocolate goodness to spoon out and enjoy when you're atop a hill, leaning on a tree, hiding in a cave… or just sitting on a sofa.

chargrilled peaches and honey

The Stranglers did a song called 'Peaches', didn't they? But it wasn't about how lovely peaches are. Oh no. It was about bums. How rude.

Serves 2

ingredients

4 peaches
Honey

method

Put the peaches on a grill, over a hot barbecue or fire embers. If they're not totally ripe in the first place, cut them in half and remove the stone before putting them on the fire. Cook until the skin blackens and the flesh softens. Then slice and pour over ridiculous amounts of honey. We suspect some cream would be good here, too.

baked berry apples

An autumnal favourite, especially if the apples have been recently hoiked from their tree and the blackberries are freshly picked. If you've got some cinnamon to hand that'd just be extra-cosy.

Serves 4

ingredients

4 cooking apples
Powdered cinnamon (optional)
2 handfuls of blackberries
Cream to serve

method

Score a line around the waist of the apple to stop it splitting and exploding. Partially core it, leaving about 1cm of apple at its base. Sprinkle over a little powdered cinnamon if you have any, then fill the hole by squishing in as many blackberries as possible. Wrap the lot in foil and rest in the embers of the campfire. Cook for 20 minutes, turning regularly.

When ready, the apple should be a golden-brown, giving up fluffy, crimson-stained flesh. Carefully unwrap and serve with lots of cream and any leftover blackberries.

baked bananas with ginger biscuits

Mmm… a crunchy, gungey, flongey, squodgy, flupperly delight. Yes, those are real words.

Serves 2

ingredients

2 bananas
4 ginger biscuits (see p139 for the recipe). Or just buy some. But you didn't hear that from us, alright?

method

Cook the bananas in their skin straight over hot coals or on a barbecue. When the skin blackens, pop the banana on a plate and carefully slice open lengthways. Scrunch up the ginger biscuits and sprinkle liberally over the hot banana.

A little peanut butter or chocolate wouldn't do any harm here, either.

popcorn

We'd just like to take this opportunity to raise a glass to the inventor of tinfoil, the late Richard Reynolds, without whom this recipe would not be possible. Cheers, Richard.

Serves 2

ingredients

50g popping corn
Olive oil

method

Make two large foil envelopes – remember that the popping corn is going to really expand and bounce around, so bigger is better.

Pour equal amounts of corn into the foil packets, along with a heavy slug of oil. Fold over and seal the edges tightly so you have a roomy package.

Rest the bag over the heat, turning occasionally with a stick or fork. After a few minutes, the corn will start to pop. As it pops, keep gently shaking the package until the popping stops.

Then, with oven-gloved hands, move the bags from the heat and carefully rip the foil open (watch out for steam). Add butter, salt or sugar to taste and eat straight from the bag.

marinated oranges

Oranges are good for you. Grand Marnier isn't. Put them together for a naughty-tasting, healthy-looking treat. These oranges are quite boozy, so don't give them to any kids unless you want Social Services on your case.

Serves 2

ingredients
6 oranges
2 shots Grand Marnier
75g dark chocolate, grated

method
Take a sharp knife and cut the top and bottom off the oranges. Now peel the skin off your central lump of orange, leaving you with a messy piece of flesh. Cut into segments over a bowl, so you catch any dribbles of juice. Add the Grand Marnier, cover and refrigerate or stick in a coolbox. When you're ready to serve, sprinkle with the chocolate shavings and tuck in.

orange-baked muffins

Did you know that by hollowing out a humble orange you get a sensational disposable cooking vessel? It's true – throw out your frying pans! You can always use pre-packaged muffin mix if you don't want to make it yourself. We won't tell.

Serves 6

ingredients

6 oranges
100g plain flour
80g butter
1 egg, beaten
80g brown sugar
80ml milk
2 tsp baking powder
1 tbsp cocoa powder

method

Cut the top off an orange and keep the 'lid' to one side. With a sharp knife, thoroughly hollow out the fruit, eating the flesh as you go. Check there are no holes elsewhere in the orange peel and plug them up with a bit of pith if there are.

To make the muffin mix, sift the flour into a bowl, add the butter, egg and brown sugar and give it a really good stir. Add the milk and baking powder, then sift the cocoa in and stir again until it has all blended in nicely. Using a whisk helps to mix it all up good and proper.

Stuff the mixture into the empty orange shells so they're about half full. Put the lid back on and wrap well with tinfoil.

When you've run out of muffin mix (or oranges), place the silver globes onto hot coals and leave for about 20 minutes, turning now and then. Don't be afraid to unwrap one carefully to check on progress. When you think they're cooked, remove from the heat and wait for them to a cool a little before you handle them. Then unwrap, discard the lid and spoon out the warm, orange-tinged muffin.

stuff we like

We've done a fair bit of cooking to get this book ship shape and between delicious gourmet meals and a few over-cooked disasters, we've discovered some very useful stuff. We suggest you leave the book open at this page, a week or so before your birthday. Maybe even circle the things you especially like the look of.

Breakdown barbecue
This amazing barbecue grill from Grilliput folds down into a neat little tube not much bigger than the size of a large cigar. www.grilliput.com

It's a skillet, innit
A skillet, like this one from Nordic Outdoor, is an easy, versatile way to cook over a campfire. www.nordicoutdoor.co.uk

Come on baby
Light My Fire offer funky mess tins and extremely useful fire starting kit. www.light-my-fire.com

Totally potty
Get some very useful lightweight titanium pots and knives from Chomette. www.chomette.co.uk

Looking sharp
These handy little penknives from Whitby & Co pack a powerful punch. www.whitbyandco.co.uk

The double-hobber
Officially known as the Campingaz Camping Chef, this 2-hob-plus-toaster set is our favourite bit of kit for longer trips, or for when the campfire police are in town. www.millets.co.uk   www.blacks.co.uk

Any time, any place
The AnyPlace range from
Fat Face includes cool-looking
tents, sleeping bags, cooking
stuff and other selected
camping paraphernalia.
www.fatface.com

Go, Jonny Go!
Check out Go! System for handy gas stoves,
lights and cooking pots.
www.rekri8.co.uk

Whizz-bang
This roaster, toaster, steamer, smoker from
Cobb is a camper's delight. There ain't nothin' it can't do. Almost.
www.cobb-bbq.co.uk

On the boil
The Eydon Kettle Company make these nifty storm
kettles for when only a brew will do.
www.eydonkettle.co.uk

What's cooking?
Talk to the nice people at Eddingtons for cast iron cookware, Dutch
ovens, portable coffee pots and this top-notch portable BBQ.
www.eddingtons.co.uk

Konichi-wa!
This is one seriously clever idea, origami plates
that fold as flat as a pancake.
www.orikaso.com

index

Share your food!

We hope you enjoyed the Cool Camping Cookbook and have learned a few new things for your next trip. If you have your own special camping recipes, why don't you share them with us? We'll credit all the recipes we receive – and the best contributions will be awarded with a free copy of the next Cool Camping Cookbook in which the recipe will be printed.

Send your recipes to **food@coolcamping.co.uk**

The Cool Camping Cookbook
Series Concept & Series Editor: Jonathan Knight
Recipes and writing: Tom Tuke-Hastings, Nadia Shireen, Shellani Gupta, Jonathan Knight
Sub-editor: Nadia Shireen
Proofreaders: Shellani Gupta, Nikki Sims
Design & Artwork: Andrew Davis
Coordinator-in-Chief: Catherine Greenwood

Published by:
Punk Publishing Ltd,
26 York Street, London W1U 6PZ

Distributed by:
Portfolio Books, Unit 5, Perivale Industrial Park, Perivale, Middlesex UB6 7RL

All photographs © Tom Tuke-Hastings and Jonathan Knight except photo p7 (courtesy of Bear Grylls), Fat Face photo p157 (courtesy of Fat Face) and the 'double-hobber' on p157 (courtesy of Campingaz).

Many of the photographs featured in this book are available for licensing. For more information, see www.coolcamping.co.uk

Thanks and love:
Big thanks to the following for help and support above and beyond the call of duty: Yurtworks (www.yurtworks.co.uk), Range Rover (www.landrover.com), Millets (www.millets.co.uk), Blacks (www.blacks.co.uk), Clever Little Ideas (www.cleverlittleideas.com), Bill Brown (www.bill-brown.com), Vango (www.vango.co.uk) and of course the boys and girls at Fat Face.

from Jonathan
This book owes so much to so many people who have contributed their time, support and enthusiasm including Bear Grylls, Keisha Willis, Max Isaac, Paul Bailey, Catherine Greenwood, Bas Greenwood, James Heraty, the guys at Shell Island, budding models Ben and Daniel Greenwood and long-suffering models/camping companions Archie and Rachel. Also, thanks to Tom for your enthusiasm for this project, to Nadia for bringing it all together and to Shellani for a virtually continuous stream of delicious food for the last few months. I owe you all lunch.

from Tom
A huge thank you to my family for all their encouragement and advice, which has been an immeasurable help. They have been heavily involved in this book and have had countless weekends disrupted by all the running around. Also, a big thank you to all the people who braved bad weather and long drives on the simple promise of something nice to eat and drink. Writing this sort of book during winter is not the easiest thing and it has been great to have friends to do it with.

Punk Publishing takes its environmental responsibilities seriously. This book has been printed on paper made from renewable sources and we continue to work with our printers to reduce our overall environmental impact. Wherever possible, we recycle, eat organic food and always turn the tap off when brushing our teeth.